GREAT ILL

SHERLOCK HOLMES

AND THE CASE OF
THE HOUND OF
THE BASKERVILLES

A. Conan Doyle

Adapted by
Malvina G. Vogel

Illustrations by Pablo Marcos Studio

BARONET
BOOKS

BARONET BOOKS, New York, New York

GREAT ILLUSTRATED CLASSICS

edited by
Malvina G. Vogel

Published by Playmore Inc., Publishers 230 Fifth Avenue, New York, N.Y. 10001 and Waldman Publishing Corp. 570 Seventh Avenue, New York, N.Y. 10018

BARONET BOOKS and the Playmore/Waldman® are registered trademarks of Playmore Inc., Publishers and Waldman Publishing Corp., New York, New York

Printed in the United States of America

Contents

About the Author

As a boy in England, Arthur Conan Doyle enjoyed reading detective stories. But once he was working his way through medical school, he didn't have much time for writing.

However, in 1886, as the twenty-seven-year-old Dr. Doyle sat in his new office hoping for patients, he decided to try writing a detective story. And so, Mr. Sherlock Holmes was born.

Over the years, Doyle himself came to be recognized as an expert on crime. He solved many real-life criminal cases and proved the innocence of men who had been imprisoned for crimes they didn't commit.

Doyle interrupted his writing career to serve as a doctor with the British Army during the Boer War in Africa. Afterwards, he had to fight the war.

For these efforts, Doyle was knighted by King Edward VII and he became Sir Arthur Conan Doyle.

During a visit to the moor country in western England, Doyle became so interested in a legend about a hound, that he used it as a plot for a new book. This book became the greatest of all of Holmes' adventures, *The Hound of the Baskervilles.*

Many of the sixty Sherlock Holmes stories have been translated into other languages and have been made even more popular in plays, movies, radio and TV.

Sir Arthur Conan Doyle died in 1930 at the age of seventy-one. But each day, the number of his readers increases, as someone discovers, for the first time, the amazing Mr. Holmes.

221B Baker Street

Characters You Will Meet

Sherlock Holmes
the most famous detective in the world

Dr. Watson
Holmes' assistant and friend

Sir Henry Baskerville
the heir to the Baskerville fortune and the
Baskerville curse

Dr. James Mortimer
a young doctor who brings the case to Sherlock

Barrymore
the mysterious butler at Baskerville Hall

Jack Stapleton
a neighbor of the Baskervilles

Beryl Stapleton
Jack's beautiful sister

Neil Selden
an escaped convict loose on the moor

Laura Lyons
a young woman trapped into becoming part of a
murderous plot

Mr. Frankland
a lawyer who lives near Baskerville Hall

Sherlock Holmes Has a Visitor.

CHAPTER 1

The Baskerville Family Legend

Mr. Sherlock Holmes was seated at his breakfast table with his back to the door when his friend, Dr. Watson, entered the room. With Watson was a tall, thin young man with a rather long nose.

"Good morning, Watson," said the famous detective without turning his head from his morning meal. "I see you have a visitor with you. Who is that tall, thin young man with a nose like a beak?"

"How did you know I had a visitor with me?" asked Watson in amazement. "I do believe you have eyes in back of your head."

Holmes laughed. "No, Watson, only a well polished silver coffeepot in front of me to serve as a mirror." Holmes turned and smiled at the young man. "And whom do I have the pleasure of greeting?" he asked.

"I am Dr. James Mortimer, Mr. Holmes. I've come to ask your help with a very unusual problem. It concerns the death of my good friend and patient, Sir Charles Baskerville."

Dr. Mortimer took a letter out of his pocket and explained, "This letter was given to me by Sir Charles just before his death three months ago. It was written by his great-greatgrandfather and has been handed down in the family from father to son for one hundred fifty years.

"Sir Charles had no children, so his entire estate plus this letter now pass to his nephew, Sir Henry Baskerville, who has been living in America for many years."

10

The Baskerville Letter

Dr. Mortimer spread out the letter for Holmes and Watson to see.

"It seems to tell about a certain legend in the Baskerville family," said Watson.

"Yes," answered Dr. Mortimer, "a legend that I believe had something to do with Sir Charles' death. If I may, I should like to read the letter to you."

Dr. Mortimer adjusted his glasses on the bridge of his nose and began to read:

"Baskerville Hall, 1742. To my sons, Rodger and John,

"The legend of the Hound of the Baskervilles has been told to me by my father who was told it by his father before him. I swear to you both that I believe the legend and so must you too.

"The legend began one hundred years ago in 1642 when this great Baskerville Hall was occupied by Hugo Baskerville—a wild, ugly, cruel man. Hugo wanted to marry the daughter of a

Dr. Mortimer Reads the Letter.

neighboring farmer, but the girl feared and hated him.

"Hugo refused to take no for an answer, and one day, with five of his evil friends, he rode to the farm and kidnapped the girl. He brought her to Baskerville Hall and locked her in an upstairs room while he and his friends had a drinking party below.

"The sounds of drunken singing and laughter reached the frantic girl. She feared for her life. She managed to escape by climbing down the ivy vines on the outside of the house. Then she fled across the dark, rocky moor towards her home.

"When Hugo discovered the girl missing, he flew into a rage. He jumped onto the table, smashing dishes under his feet and swearing to give his body and soul to the devil if he could catch the girl.

"But only his trained hounds could hope to find anything or anyone out on the dark moor.

Hugo Kidnaps the Girl.

Hugo gave them her scent from a kerchief she had left behind, and then he let them loose, trailing them on his black mare.

"His friends joined the chase too, until a strange sight stopped them cold. Ahead, at the top of a hill, stood Hugo's hounds. These usually brave animals were whimpering in fear and slinking away from the valley below.

"The riders headed for the hilltop and stared down. At first, all they could see were the piles of tall stones put there by ancient moor people thousands of years ago. Then the moon came out from behind the clouds and lit up the foot of the stones. There lay two bodies—Hugo's and the girl's. Standing over Hugo's body was a huge black beast tearing out his throat.

"The hound turned its blazing eyes and bloody jaws towards the riders who screamed in terror and went mad instantly.

The Legend of the Hound Begins.

"This, my sons, is the legend of the hound that has brought evil to our family. For since that tragic day, many Baskervilles have been cursed with sudden, bloody, and mysterious deaths out on the moor.

"So I write this letter to warn you. Do not cross the moor alone at night! For somewhere out on that dark rocky hillside, the hound is waiting to claim your lives too."

When Dr. Mortimer finished reading, he stared at Holmes. The detective yawned.

"Didn't you find the letter interesting?" asked Dr. Mortimer.

"Not especially," said Holmes. "I really don't like fairy tales."

"But Mr. Holmes," cried Dr. Mortimer, "surely Sir Charles Baskerville's death was not a fairy-tale!"

"Well, then, suppose you tell us exactly how Sir Charles died," urged Holmes.

Holmes Doesn't Like Fairy Tales.

"The facts are simple," began Dr. Mortimer. "Sir Charles had a habit of taking a walk every night along Yew Alley, a path on the grounds of Baskerville Hall. He never went out on the moor at night because he was too frightened of the legend.

"One night, when Sir Charles didn't return from his walk, his butler, Barrymore, became alarmed. He went out after him and found his body at the end of Yew Alley.

"When I arrived at Baskerville Hall, I was able to follow Sir Charles' footprints along Yew Alley because it was rather muddy from an all-day rain. Halfway down the path, there is a gate that opens onto the moor. I believe that Sir Charles stopped at the gate during his walk, for when I checked the ground there, I found a fresh pile of ashes from his cigar.

"But something about those footprints puzzles me. From the house to the moor gate, Sir Charles left whole footprints. But from the moor gate to

Ashes at the Moor Gate

the spot where he died, the prints looked as if he were walking on his tiptoes.

"When I reached Sir Charles' body, he was face down. But his face was so twisted that, at first, I barely recognized him. Then I found something nearby—something so frightening that I didn't even report it to the police because I . . ."

"Never mind why," interrupted Holmes. "What was it you found?"

"Other footprints!" exclaimed Dr. Mortimer. "Fresh clear footprints!"

"Were they a man's or a woman's?" asked Holmes.

Dr. Mortimer looked from Holmes to Watson. His face turned white and his lips trembled as he gasped, "They were the footprints of a gigantic hound!"

The Hound's Footprints!

The Hound on the Moor

CHAPTER 2

Dr. Mortimer's Problem

"A gigantic hound?" asked Holmes and Watson together.

Dr. Mortimer nodded. "I am certain that it was the very same ugly black beast I had been seeing out on the moor near Baskerville Hall when I visited Sir Charles. The beast gave off such a strange light that I thought at times I was seeing a supernatural creature. When I finally told Sir Charles what I had been seeing, he told me of the legend, then gave me the letter which I just read to you."

"Very well," said Holmes, "but what exactly is it that you want me to do?"

"First," said Dr. Mortimer, "I need you to advise me what to do with Sir Henry Baskerville, who is arriving here today."

Holmes rubbed his chin and thought a moment. "Is Sir Henry the only heir to the Baskerville estate?" he asked.

"Yes," answered Dr. Mortimer. "Sir Charles had two younger brothers—James and Rodger. James was Sir Henry's father—a kind, generous man who died several years ago. Rodger was very much like old Hugo of the legend—wild, ugly and cruel. He got himself into a great deal of trouble with the law here in England, so he fled to South America where he died of yellow fever. As far as we know, Rodger never married and never had any children.

"So you see, Mr. Holmes, Sir Henry is the last of the Baskervilles, and I simply do not know where to take him."

Sir Henry, the Last of the Baskervilles

"Why not to his family home?" asked Holmes.

"I'm afraid to," said Dr. Mortimer, "because every Baskerville who goes there meets with an evil, mysterious death."

Holmes thought for a few moments, then said, "If someone or something is trying to kill off the Baskervilles, I don't think Sir Henry would be safe anywhere—not at Baskerville Hall and not here in London."

"So what do you suggest, Mr. Holmes?" asked Dr. Mortimer.

"I would suggest that you meet Sir Henry at the station and take him to a hotel. But say nothing to him about this matter until I have had time to think about it. Then, tomorrow morning at ten o'clock, bring him here to Baker Street to see me."

"I will do what you say," said Dr. Mortimer as he rose to leave. "And thank you."

Dr. Mortimer Thanks Sherlock Holmes.

"Well, what do you make of it, Holmes?" asked Watson after the door had closed behind Dr. Mortimer.

"Much of it is very confusing," said Holmes, already deep in thought.

"Especially the change in footprints," said Watson. "Why would Sir Charles have walked on his toes down Yew Alley after he passed the moor gate?"

"But he didn't walk on his toes," exclaimed Holmes. "He was running, Watson, running for his life, running until his heart gave out and he fell dead."

"But running from what?" asked Watson.

"From something that frightened him while he was standing at the moor gate smoking his cigar," explained Holmes. "Why, Watson, I believe that Sir Charles was so terrified by what he had seen that he lost all his reason. Remember, he ran *away* from the house into the darkness instead of *towards* the house for safety."

Sir Charles Runs for His Life.

"But why do you suppose he stopped at the gate at all?" asked Watson.

"I believe Sir Charles was waiting for someone out there," said Holmes. "But the question is why and who. After all, the man was old and sickly. I can understand his taking a walk after dinner on a pleasant evening, but this was a wet, rainy night, hardly the kind of night for a stroll in the garden. No, Watson, I am certain that Sir Charles was out there to meet someone. But, my dear fellow, that is all we know for now. Perhaps we shall discover more when we meet Sir Henry Baskerville tomorrow morning."

Was Sir Charles Meeting Someone?

Holmes Welcomes Sir Henry Baskerville.

CHAPTER 3

Sir Henry Baskerville

At ten the next morning, Dr. Mortimer arrived at 221B Baker Street with a handsome, dark-haired young man of about thirty in a brown tweed suit and matching hat.

"This is Sir Henry Baskerville," said Dr. Mortimer as they entered.

"Please sit down, Sir Henry," said Sherlock Holmes. "Watson and I are honored."

"Gentlemen," began Sir Henry, "I am delighted that Dr. Mortimer brought me here to see the world's greatest detective, even though he hasn't told me why. You see, I received a rather puzzling letter at my hotel a short while ago, and I don't know if it's a joke or something serious."

"May we see it, Sir Henry?" asked Watson.

Sir Henry took an envelope out of his jacket pocket and laid it on the table. Holmes and Watson studied the plain grey envelope. It was addressed with ink in rough, printed letters to "SIR HENRY BASKERVILLE, NORTHUMBERLAND HOTEL, LONDON." The postmark was dated just last evening.

"Who knew you were going to the Northumberland Hotel?" asked Holmes.

"No one could have known," answered Sir Henry. "We only decided where to stay after I met Dr. Mortimer."

"Hmm! So, someone is very interested in your movements," said Holmes as he opened the envelope and took out a folded piece of paper. He spread the paper flat on the table and stared at the cut-out words pasted across it—"IF YOU

Sir Henry's Mysterious Letter

VALUE YOUR LIFE, KEEP AWAY FROM THE MOOR." Only the word "moor" was printed in ink.

"Now Mr. Holmes," said Sir Henry, "can you tell me what that letter means?"

"Give me a few minutes to examine this letter, Sir Henry." Holmes turned to Watson and asked, "Do we still have yesterday's *London Times*?"

Watson handed the newspaper to Holmes who turned the pages and ran his eyes up and down the columns.

"Halloa! What's this?" exclaimed Holmes as his finger stopped at a story on an inside page. "Here, my dear Watson, is the very story from which the words in the note were cut. See, here's the 'if,' the 'you,' the 'value,' the 'your,' the 'life.' And here's the 'keep away' and the 'from the.'"

"By thunder, Holmes, you're right!" cried Watson.

A Puzzling Message

"Very clever of you, Mr. Holmes," said Sir Henry, "but how do you explain that the word 'moor' was written and not pasted?"

"Probably because 'moor' could not be found in print," answered Holmes. "It is not as common a word as all the others."

"Really, Mr. Holmes, you are amazing!" said Dr. Mortimer. "I could understand anyone figuring out that the words came from a newspaper, but how did you know it was the *London Times*?"

"My dear doctor," answered Holmes, "just as you are able to tell the difference between the spots from measles and those from smallpox, so I have trained myself to know the different styles of type used in different newspapers. Then too, since the letter was postmarked with yesterday's date, I felt certain that the words were cut from yesterday's paper. Also, my trained eye has found another clue that the writer has tried to hide. Since the printing of the address is in rough

"How Did You Know It Was the *Times*?"

letters, it shows that the writer wanted to hide his real handwriting. So I would guess that the writer is someone you already know or someone you will get to know soon."

Sir Henry and Dr. Mortimer looked at Holmes in amazement. What a clever mind!

Holmes went on. "Look, too, at how the words are pasted on. They are not in a straight line. Some are higher than others. That tells me that the writer must have been in a great hurry. If that is so, the question is why. Perhaps the writer was afraid that someone else would discover the letter while he was writing it."

"Now aren't you just guessing, Mr. Holmes?" asked Dr. Mortimer.

"Sir," answered Holmes firmly, "a detective must often make guesses and then check out the ones that seem the most likely."

The Writer Was in a Great Hurry.

Holmes picked up the letter again and brought it up close to his eyes. He lifted his eyebrows as if something about the letter surprised him.

"Have you found something?" asked Watson.

"Nothing yet," said Holmes as he put the paper down. Then he turned to Sir Henry and asked, "Well now, has anything else unusual happened to you since your arrival?"

"Why no," said Sir Henry, "unless you consider losing one of my boots unusual."

"I'm sure you just misplaced it in your room, Sir Henry," said Dr. Mortimer. "We don't have to bother Mr. Holmes with such an unimportant matter."

"Nothing is unimportant during an investigation," snapped Holmes. "Now suppose you tell me what happened, Sir Henry."

"I simply put my brown boots outside my door last night so that the porter could polish them. When I awoke this morning, one was gone. I

Another Clue in the Letter?

suppose I'm especially upset for I had just bought the boots yesterday, and I never even wore them."

"If they were new, why did they have to be polished?" asked Holmes.

"The leather had a dull finish and I wanted them shinier," said Sir Henry.

"It doesn't make much sense for someone to steal just one boot," said Holmes. He seemed deep in thought for a moment, then added, "but it will probably turn up soon."

That seemed to make Sir Henry feel better. "Well, now that the matter of the boot is out of the way, I think it's time for someone to tell me why Dr. Mortimer has brought me here and why Mr. Holmes has been asking me all these questions."

Dr. Mortimer looked at Holmes. At a nod from the detective, Dr. Mortimer took the Baskerville letter from his pocket and began the story of the family hound.

One Boot Is Gone!

When he had finished, Sir Henry smiled. "I have been hearing this story of the hound ever since I was a small child, but I have never taken it very seriously. Are you saying now that this pasted letter has something to do with the hound story?"

"I'm not quite sure," said Holmes, "but it is obvious that someone is trying to warn you of some danger at Baskerville Hall."

"Nonsense!" cried Sir Henry. "I refuse to believe that I am in any danger, either from this family hound or from any human being. Now, if you'll excuse me, Mr. Holmes, I think that Dr. Mortimer and I shall take a pleasant walk back to our hotel. Suppose you and Dr. Watson join us there for lunch. Say at two o'clock?"

"Thank you, Sir Henry," said Holmes. "We shall be there."

As Watson showed the two men out, Holmes walked quickly over to the window.

A Child's Story!

"That's Our Man, Watson!"

The instant he heard the door close behind them, he rushed for his coat, calling to Watson to do the same.

"We haven't a moment to lose, Watson," cried Holmes as they hurried down the stairs and out into the street. Sir Henry and Dr. Mortimer were nearing the corner.

"Shall I run and stop them?" asked Watson.

"Not for the world, my dear fellow," said Holmes. "They must not see us."

Holmes and Watson followed half a block behind Sir Henry and Dr. Mortimer. When the two men stopped to look in a shop window, Holmes and Watson did the same.

Suddenly, Holmes gave a cry, "Halloa! What have we here?"

Watson followed Holmes' eye and saw that a carriage had stopped when they stopped.

"That's our man, Watson!" exclaimed Holmes. "Let's try to get a look at him."

They stepped into the road and started across. Through a side window of the carriage, they spied a man with a bushy black beard and light hair.

When the man saw them approaching, he screamed to the driver, and the carriage dashed wildly down the street. Within moments, it was out of sight.

"Blast our luck!" muttered Holmes angrily. "That man has probably been following Sir Henry since he arrived in London. I guessed that Sir Henry was being followed when he showed us that pasted letter he received at his hotel. Otherwise, how would anyone know where he was staying? I also guessed that he'd be followed today too. And when I looked out the window as Sir Henry and Dr. Mortimer were leaving, I saw that carriage parked just down the street."

"Marvelous!" cried Watson. "Now we can trace that man through the carriage driver." Then

The Stranger Escapes.

Watson's face fell. "But we didn't get the carriage number."

"My dear Watson," said Holmes, "I may have been clumsy in letting the man escape, but surely you can't believe that I'd miss the carriage number. It's 2704."

"Amazing, Holmes!" cried Watson.

"Did you get a good look at the man's face?" asked Holmes.

"I only noticed the beard," said Watson.

"So did I," agreed Holmes. "And it was probably a fake one. A clever man would use it to hide his real face. And now, Watson, since Dr. Mortimer and Sir Henry are already out of sight, we shall busy ourselves trying to locate the driver of carriage number 2704 before we keep our lunch date at the Northumberland Hotel."

Holmes Gets the Carriage Number.

A Different Boot Is Missing!

CHAPTER 4

Two Dead Ends

Promptly at two o'clock, Holmes and Watson knocked at the door to Sir Henry's hotel room. When Sir Henry opened the door, he held an old dusty black boot in his hand. His face was red with anger.

"I don't know what's going on in this hotel," he screamed, "but now another boot is missing. This time, it's one of my old black ones. Oh dear, Mr. Holmes, I am sorry for troubling you about such unimpor . . . ."

"Oh, but it is worth troubling me about," interrupted Holmes. "I never overlook anything that might turn out to be a clue. I also must inform you that I now have proof that you are being followed here in London. In a city so large, it is difficult to discover who is following you and why, so I think you ought to go to Baskerville Hall as soon as possible."

"Sir Henry followed?" cried Dr. Mortimer. "But by whom?"

"All I know is the man has a bushy black beard," said Holmes. "Do you know anyone with such a beard, Dr. Mortimer?"

Dr. Mortimer thought a moment. "Why yes," he said slowly. "Barrymore, the butler."

"Aha!" cried Holmes. "And where is Barrymore now?"

"He should be at Baskerville Hall preparing for Sir Henry's arrival."

"We had better make sure he is there and not here in London," said Holmes. "What you must do, Dr. Mortimer, is send off a telegram to Mr. Barrymore. Simply ask him if everything is ready

Holmes Describes the Stranger.

for Sir Henry's arrival. Then send off another one to the postmaster at the telegraph office. Tell him that Mr. Barrymore's telegram must be delivered to Mr. Barrymore, himself, and to no one else. Also tell him that if Mr. Barrymore is not at home, the wire is to be returned to you at the hotel immediately."

After Dr. Mortimer left to send the two telegrams, Sir Henry turned to Holmes and asked, "Do you really believe that Barrymore might be trying to scare me away? Why, his family has been looking after Baskerville Hall for almost one hundred years!"

"My dear fellow," began Holmes, "this Barrymore and his wife have a very fine home at Baskerville Hall. Perhaps they fear that a new owner will want new servants. Anyway, Sir Henry, I believe that you should start for the Hall immediately. But you must not go alone."

Sending Off Two Telegrams

"Dr. Mortimer will be with me."

Holmes shook his head. "Dr. Mortimer has his practice to attend to. Besides, he lives miles away from the Hall. No, someone must be with you at all times."

"Can't you come with me, Mr. Holmes?"

"At the moment, I am still working on a case here in London, Sir Henry," explained Holmes. "But I have great trust in my friend, Dr. Watson. He shall go with you. You will surely feel safe with him around."

Watson looked surprised for the moment, but before he could say a word, Sir Henry took his hand and shook it hard. "Thank you, Dr. Watson," he said. "You are so kind."

"Fine! That settles it," said Holmes. "You both should be ready to leave by tomorrow. So we shall meet at the station for the 10:30 train."

Holmes and Watson were getting up to leave when Sir Henry gave a cry and made a dive for

Sir Henry Thanks Dr. Watson.

the floor under a cabinet. "My missing boot!" he cried as he stood up with the new brown boot in his hand. "But I searched this room, every inch of it!"

"Well, at least one of our problems is solved," said Holmes, but a puzzled expression remained on his face. How odd that the boot turned up in a spot that had already been searched!

Holmes was silent all during the ride home, and he spent most of the afternoon sitting, smoking his pipe, and thinking.

Just before dinner, a messenger arrived with a note from Sir Henry. It read: "DR. MORTIMER JUST RECEIVED WORD THAT BARRYMORE IS AT BASKERVILLE HALL. SIGNED, SIR HENRY."

"That's a dead end for one of my clues, Watson," said Holmes. "But we still have one clue left—the carriage driver. His office said they would send him around this afternoon."

The First Missing Boot Turns Up.

Just then, the bell rang, and a rough-looking man appeared at the door.

"You the gent what's been askin' for the driver of cab 2704?" he asked.

"Yes, yes! Come in, my good man," said Holmes. "I'd like you to tell me anything you can about the man who hired you to drive him here to watch this house about ten o'clock this morning, then had you follow two men who left here."

The man looked surprised. "You seem to know as much as I do, sir," he said. "All I can add is that the man told me he was a detective and I wasn't to speak to anyone about him."

"Did he say anything more?" asked Holmes.

"He told me his name."

Holmes smiled at Watson. Perhaps they were going to have some luck after all.

"And what was the name he told you, my good man?" asked Holmes confidently.

The Driver of Carriage 2704

"His name," said the driver, "was Mr. Sherlock Holmes!"

Holmes thanked the driver, then showed him out. "This is a very clever man we're dealing with, Watson. He followed Sir Henry here and realized we were on the case. He also probably recognized me when we got close to his carriage. He knew I would be clever enough to get the carriage number and question the driver. By sending back the message that he was 'Sherlock Holmes,' he was playing a sly game with us."

"So we reached another dead end," said Watson. "I certainly hope I have better luck at Baskerville Hall."

"Yes," said Holmes, "but I must admit I'll worry about you. This is dangerous business, and I shall be very happy when I see you safely back here once more."

Another Dead End!

First Glimpse of the Moor!

CHAPTER 5

Baskerville Hall

As the 10:30 train sped towards the countryside, Sir Henry gazed at the rich green fields where he had spent his childhood. The pleasant memories brought a smile to his face. But then the moor came into view—the grey, rocky, gloomy hills that were now a danger to him. He shuddered.

Dr. Mortimer, who was familiar enough with the countryside, turned his gaze to Sir Henry. The young man certainly had the proud look of the Baskerville men, even though his American clothes and his American way of speaking seemed out of place.

Dr. Watson was thinking back to Sherlock Holmes' last-minute instructions. He was never to leave Sir Henry alone outside the Hall. And he was to learn all he could about the neighbors: Dr. Mortimer and his wife; Mr. and Mrs. Barrymore, who worked at the Hall; the Stapletons— the brother, Jack, who spent his time studying plant and animal life, and his beautiful sister, Beryl, who helped him in his work; and Mr. Frankland, an elderly lawyer who lived alone and who was rather strange in his ways.

These people all must be studied to see if any of them could be behind this strange plot. Watson felt for the revolver hidden under his jacket. That, at least, made him feel a little more comfortable.

The train pulled into the small neat country station of Coombe Tracey and the three men got off. Watson looked around. Off to a side stood two

Watson Feels for His Revolver.

uniformed men armed "with rifles. They studied the three new arrivals curiously.

As soon as the luggage was loaded onto a carriage and everyone was seated, the driver started off down the wide white road. Rolling green pasture lands flew by, and old gabled houses peeked out through thick green trees.

But behind the peaceful countryside rose the long gloomy curve of the moor. Its sharp, rocky, evil-looking hills seemed to be sending out a warning to the visitors.

As the carriage turned off onto a side road, Dr. Mortimer cried, "Halloa! What's this?"

A soldier, mounted on his horse, was staring down at them from a hill on the moor. The driver turned in his seat and explained, "There's been an escape from Princetown jail, sir, and the guards are watching every road and every station. And it isn't just an ordinary convict that's escaped, sir. It's that insane, throat-cutting Neil Selden, the Notting Hill murderer."

Arriving at Coombe Tracey

The three men felt a chill of fear run through them. Now there was an added danger out there on the moor—a murderer.

Just then, the carriage reached the top of a hill, and the driver pointed with his whip at two tall, narrow, black towers rising from the clumps of bent, twisted trees in the valley. "Baskerville Hall!" he said.

A few minutes later, the carriage entered a long dark tunnel formed by the branches on either side of the road. At the end of this tunnel stood a large black building. Candles glimmering in the windows gave it an almost ghostly look.

Sir Henry looked around uncomfortably. "This place is enough to scare any man," he said, "especially one as old as my uncle."

"Welcome, Sir Henry! Welcome to Baskerville Hall!" came a voice from the doorway.

A tall man with a black beard came out to "open the carriage door. A woman followed behind to help unload the luggage.

"Baskerville Hall!"

Dr. Mortimer kept his luggage on board and explained, "I shall drive straight home as my wife is expecting me. I'm sure that the Barrymores will show you around the Hall, Sir Henry. So, goodbye for now."

Watson and Sir Henry entered Baskerville Hall. The door clanged heavily behind them.

"It's just as I imagined it," said Sir Henry as he gazed at the tall stained-glass windows, the dark oak paneling, and the family portraits on the wall. "To think that this is the very same house in which my people have lived for centuries!"

Just then, Barrymore announced that their rooms were ready. Watson was relieved when he saw that his room was next to Sir Henry's.

Before going to bed, Watson opened his window and looked out onto the moor. The cold jagged rocks shone dimly in the light of the half-moon. Even the clouds seemed to be racing across the sky to escape the dangers on the moor.

Sir Henry Is Home at Last!

The house was filled with a deathly silence, broken only by the chiming clock as it struck the quarter hour.

Then, suddenly in the dead of night, came the sobs of a woman followed by a strange strangling gasp. Watson sat up in bed and listened.

He waited, frozen in that position for almost an hour. But the only sound that followed was the chiming of the clock and the rustling of the trees outside the house.

Watson Hears Strange Sounds.

Sir Henry Questions Barrymore.

CHAPTER 6

The Stapletons of Merripit House

At breakfast the next morning, Watson discovered that Sir Henry had heard the noises during the night too. They decided to check further.

Sir Henry called Barrymore in and asked him what he knew about the woman's cries. The butler trembled and turned pale. But he denied that the cries had come from his wife.

However, a few minutes later, when Mrs. Barrymore came in to clear off the table, her eyes were red and swollen. So, Barrymore was lying, thought Watson. But why? Could he be lying about other things too? Perhaps he really was the bearded man in the carriage in London. Watson decided to check further.

So off he went to the telegraph office in Coombe Tracey. There, he learned that the wire Dr. Mortimer had sent from London was actually handed to Mrs. Barrymore. Was her husband really busy working upstairs as she had told the messenger or was she lying for him? And why did he lie about his wife's cries? Was he trying to frighten off Sir Henry? Watson was puzzling over these questions as he walked back to Baskerville Hall.

Suddenly, his thoughts were interrupted by the sound of running feet and a breathless voice calling his name. Watson turned and saw a thin, light-haired man coming towards him. The man carried a butterfly net in his hand, and a box with flower and leaf samples hung from his shoulder.

Watson Checks on the Telegrams.

"Dr. Watson," gasped the breathless man, "here on the moor, we are friendly people. We do not wait to be introduced. I am Jack Stapleton of Merripit House. Dr. Mortimer has told me all about you."

"How do you do," said Watson.

"I do hope that Sir Henry is well after his long journey," said Stapleton. "I must admit that I am surprised he hasn't been frightened off by the stories about the hound."

"I really don't think he believes it," said Watson.

"But you must know that the peasants living here swear to it," said Stapleton. "Some even claim to have seen the hound. Why, I, for one, believe that Sir Charles saw the hound the night he died. And that is what frightened him and led to his heart attack. Tell me, Dr. Watson, is that what Mr. Sherlock Holmes thinks too?"

Watson Meets Jack Stapleton.

Watson caught his breath. This fellow seems to know a great deal about me and about Holmes, he thought.

But Stapleton didn't seem to notice Watson's surprise. Without waiting for Watson's answer, Stapleton continued, "And is the famous Mr. Holmes joining you here?"

"He cannot leave London right now," said Watson. "He's still busy on another case."

The path they were following branched off, and Stapleton pointed to the right, explaining, "This path takes us to Merripit House. Would you care to join me there and meet my sister?"

Watson remembered Holmes' instructions about gathering as much information as possible about the neighbors, so he smiled and followed Stapleton down the path.

"The moor is a wonderful place," said Stapleton as he pointed to the sharp jagged rocks sticking up. "It holds many strange secrets on its bare hills. And I should know, for I have explored most

"The Moor Is a Wonderful Place."

of the countryside around here. For example, look over at that plain to the north."

Watson's eyes followed in the direction Stapleton was pointing. "Why, that bright green grass looks like a fine place to take a horse for a gallop!" he said.

Stapleton laughed. "Those bright green patches of grass have cost many men and beasts their lives. For that is the great Grimpen Mire. One step onto that grass and the soft deep mud just below it pulls any living thing down into it and to death."

"Amazing!" exclaimed Watson.

"But I am the only person who can walk across the mire safely," boasted Stapleton, "because I know the exact grass patches that have hard ground beneath them."

Just then, a wild pony came galloping across the moor heading towards the mire. On his first

The Deadly Grimpen Mire!

step into the soft grass-covered mud, he began sinking. His neck shot up as his body twisted. A dreadful cry came from his slowly disappearing head, and then the pony was gone.

Watson watched in horror, but Stapleton simply shrugged. "This happens almost every day in this place," he said calmly.

The next instant, a long, low moan swept over the moor. It started low, then grew into a roar, then sank back into a moan.

Watson stood frozen. A chill of fear went through him. "What was that?" he cried.

"The peasants around here say it is the Hound of the Baskervilles calling for its next victim," replied Stapleton grimly.

"Come, come now, Stapleton," protested Watson. "You are an educated man. Surely you don't believe in such nonsense."

"A man may get to believe anything when he lives on the moor," said Stapleton. "In fact,

The Mire Claims Another Victim.

Watson, look over there on that steep slope. See those rings of grey stone? They are huts built by prehistoric men who lived on the moor thousands of years ago. No one has disturbed those huts since then. Oh, excuse me. There goes a Cyclopides!"

A small fly had fluttered in front of Stapleton, and he rushed after it with his net held high. Watson caught his breath as he saw the fly heading towards the great mire, but Stapleton never stopped for an instant. He jumped from one grass patch to another, zig-zagging over the mud as if he were on hard solid ground.

As Watson stood admiring the little man flitting about, the sound of footsteps behind him made him turn around. A beautiful young woman was coming up the path. This must be Stapleton's sister, Beryl, he thought. But she didn't look anything like him. Jack Stapleton was short, fair-skinned, and light-haired, while his sister was

Stapleton Crosses the Mire Safely.

tall, dark-skinned, and with the blackest hair Watson had ever seen. In her elegant dress, she seemed almost out of place here on the moor.

Watson raised his hat and started to greet her when the young woman cried out, "Go back! Go back to London this minute!"

Watson stared at her in shock. "Why should I go back?" he asked.

"I cannot explain," she whispered, "but for God's sake, go away and never set foot on the moor again! Now hush. My brother is coming back. Not a word of what I said."

As Stapleton approached, his sister began talking about the flowers on the moor.

"Halloa Beryl!" called Stapleton, breathing hard from the chase. He glanced suspiciously from his sister to Watson. "So, you two have already met?"

"Yes, Jack," she answered. "I was telling Sir Henry about our moor flowers."

Beryl Stapleton's Warning!

"Sir Henry?" asked Stapleton, puzzled.

"Yes, Sir Henry Baskerville," she said.

"No, no," answered Watson. "I'm not Sir Henry. I'm his friend, Dr. Watson."

The young woman's face turned red and she lowered her eyes to hide her embarrassment. Stapleton then suggested that they head back to Merripit House. Watson agreed.

During the visit, Jack Stapleton told Watson how he and his sister had come to the country after a school he had run in Yorkshire had failed. Here, on the moor, they spent their time studying nature.

At one point, when Stapleton left the room to bring Watson some samples from his butterfly collection, Beryl Stapleton leaned forward and whispered, "I must talk quickly before my brother returns. Please forget what I said to you earlier."

"But Miss Stapleton," said Watson, "I can't forget it or the fear in your eyes when you spoke. I

Stapleton Talks About Himself.

care what happens to Sir Henry, so please tell me why you want him to return to London."

"Because my bro . . ." Then she stopped. "Because the moor brings evil to his family."

"I feel there's more that you're not telling me," said Watson. "If you're only worried about the stories of the hound, why didn't you want your brother to know what we were talking about?"

The woman looked terrified. "I cannot tell you any more," she cried as she ran from the room.

Watson left soon after. As he made his way back to Baskerville Hall, he was filled with new fears as the mystery deepened.

Beryl Stapleton's Mysterious Secret!

Watson Begins His Report.

CHAPTER 7

Dr. Watson's Report

Baskerville Hall
October 15th

MY DEAR HOLMES,—

In the two weeks that I have been here, this case has become even stranger than it was before. But I shall report all that has happened and let you judge for yourself.

First of all, Sir Henry has been showing a great interest in our beautiful neighbor, Miss Stapleton. She has been enjoying his attention, but I'm not quite sure how her brother feels about it.

Yesterday was a perfect example. After breakfast, Sir Henry put on his hat and coat and prepared to go out. Following your instructions not to let him go out alone, I picked up my hat and coat too.

Sir Henry looked at me in a curious way and asked if I was coming with him.

"If you are going to the moor," I told him, "the answer is yes. You know my instructions from Holmes."

"My dear fellow," said Sir Henry with his hand on my shoulder, "you understand that I am going out to meet a young lady. Surely, when Holmes gave you those orders, he could not have known that I would fall in love."

Before I had a chance to say another word, Sir Henry had picked up his walking stick and was gone. I knew I had a responsibility, so I set out after him.

When I reached the top of the hill, I saw Sir Henry walking side by side on the moor with

Sir Henry Wants to Go Out Alone.

Miss Stapleton. I couldn't decide whether to follow them and be rude, or watch from where I was. But before I could make up my mind, I suddenly realized that I was not the only one watching them. My eye caught the movement of a butterfly net, and then I saw Jack Stapleton running wildly towards them.

I could not hear what they were saying, but Stapleton seemed to be raging at Sir Henry, while Sir Henry seemed to be trying to calm him. Finally, Stapleton took his sister's arm and pulled her with him towards their house.

Sir Henry watched them go, then slowly turned back up the hill. As he came towards me, he didn't even appear angry at me for having followed him. Instead, he asked me a rather strange question.

"Watson, did that brother of hers ever strike you as being crazy?"

Stapleton Is Enraged!

I had never thought of Jack Stapleton as crazy and I told him so. But Sir Henry was completely puzzled. Why would Stapleton object so strongly to their meeting on the moor? Why did his sister keep warning Sir Henry of the danger he was in? And why did Stapleton become even more enraged when Sir Henry had asked permission to marry his sister? Sir Henry couldn't understand it, and I'm afraid I couldn't either.

But later that afternoon, Stapleton came to the Hall to apologize to Sir Henry. He admitted that it would be selfish of him to stop his sister from marrying a fine man like Sir Henry. He asked only that Sir Henry promise to call upon his sister for three months so they could get to know each other better. This pleased Sir Henry, but still left me somewhat suspicious.

I have also met the other neighbor, Mr. Frankland of Lafter Hall, an elderly lawyer. He has

Stapleton Apologizes to Sir Henry.

been living alone for several years since his only daughter ran off to get married. Frankland is quite fond of astronomy and has an excellent telescope on the roof of his house. He has been using that telescope lately to look up and down the moor, in the hope of spotting that escaped convict.

I have saved the most important news for last. It concerns the Barrymores. After my visit to the telegraph office, I told Sir Henry that Barrymore had not received the telegram himself. When Sir Henry questioned him, Barrymore explained that his wife had accepted it because he was busy and that she had also answered it when he told her what to write.

Barrymore was quite upset to being questioned and accused Sir Henry of not trusting him. Sir Henry tried to convince him that this was not so. He even gave Barrymore a gift of all the clothing

Mr. Frankland Searches the Moor.

he had brought with him from America now that all the new things he bought in London have arrived.

Anyway, that night, Sir Henry and I were sitting in his room puzzling over this situation. At about 2:00 A.M., just as I was preparing to leave, we heard footsteps outside in the hall. We opened the door quietly and peered out. There was Barrymore walking down the long hall with a candle in his hand.

We tiptoed out and followed him. He turned the corner and entered a room at the end of another long hall. The rooms at that side of the house are all empty, so we couldn't understand why he was there.

We saw him crouch down at the window and hold the candle against the glass.

At that moment, Sir Henry walked noisily into the room. Barrymore jumped away from the window and turned towards us. His face was white, and his dark eyes full of fear.

Sir Henry Gives Barrymore a Gift.

"What are you doing here, Barrymore?" demanded Sir Henry.

"N-n-nothing, sir," he answered. The candle was shaking in his hand. "I was just checking to see that all the windows were closed."

"That's a lie!" cried Sir Henry sharply. "Why were you holding the candle in the window?"

Barrymore looked helpless. "Please don't ask me, Sir Henry," he begged. "I give you my word it has nothing to do with you at all."

But I had another idea, Holmes. Since that window faced the moor, I decided that Barrymore must have been holding that candle as a signal. I had to see if someone out there was answering. So I took the candle from Barrymore and walked over to the window. I held it against the glass as he had done. Soon a tiny dot of yellow light appeared out on the moor.

The Candle in the Window

"Now who is your partner out there?" I demanded. "And what are you up to, Barrymore?"

"It's my business and nobody else's," said Barrymore stubbornly. "I will not tell."

"Then you must leave my home right away," said Sir Henry bitterly. "I cannot have you living and working here when you are plotting against my life."

"Oh no, sir, not against you!" came a voice from the doorway. It was a pale and frightened Mrs. Barrymore. "I fear that this is all my fault for my husband was just helping me, or rather my brother."

"Your brother?" asked Sir Henry.

"Yes, sir," she said. "My brother is out there on the moor starving. The light is a signal that we are bringing food to him. And his light is to show us where he is."

"Who is your brother?" asked Sir Henry.

Mrs. Barrymore Confesses.

"My brother," answered the sobbing woman, "is . . . Neil Selden, the escaped convict. So you see, sir, this is not a plot against you. Neil always looked to me for help ever since he was a child. So when he crawled here one night several weeks ago, weary and starving, I had to take him in and feed him and care for him. Then you came to the Hall, sir, and he went to hide on the moor. Please don't blame my husband, Sir Henry. He was only doing it for me."

Sir Henry turned to Barrymore. "Is this true?" he asked.

"Every word, sir!" he replied.

"Well, I cannot blame you for helping your wife," said Sir Henry. "Forget what I said about leaving. Go to your room and we shall discuss this further in the morning."

After the servants left, Sir Henry and I gazed out the window.

"A Murderer Is Out There on the Moor!"

"A murderer is out there on the moor," he cried, "and we don't know where he might strike next. By thunder, I am going out to catch that man!"

"I will come with you," I said.

We went for our coats and I tucked my revolver inside my jacket. Within minutes, we were out the door and on our way down Yew Alley towards the moor gate.

No sooner had we passed the gate than a strange cry sounded in the night. It was a long, deep moan that rose to a loud roar, then died away. Again and again it sounded.

Sir Henry grabbed my sleeve. His face was white. "My God, Watson, what was that?"

I tried not to alarm him. "It's just a sound they have on the moor."

"Watson," groaned Sir Henry, "that was the cry of the hound—the one they call the Hound of the Baskervilles. My God, can there be some truth to all those stories? Is it possible that my life really

Sir Henry Hears the Cry of the Hound!

is in danger from this hound? You don't believe it, do you, Watson?"

"No, no, Sir Henry! Certainly not!"

But Sir Henry was not convinced. "It was one thing to laugh about the story in London," he said, "but it is another thing to stand here on the moor and hear such a dreadful cry. And my uncle! There were footprints of a hound near his body. It all fits together. Oh, Watson, I have never been a coward in my life, but that cry seemed to freeze my blood."

I then suggested that we return to the house, but Sir Henry wouldn't hear of it.

"We came to get our man, Watson, and, by thunder, we will do it."

We started climbing the rocks on the hillside until we reached the rock on which the candle stood. We hid behind a large boulder and waited for Selden.

Suddenly, from behind a rock on the other side of the candle, a face appeared. It was an evil

Waiting for a Murderer

yellow face that looked almost as if it belonged to an animal. A mass of tangled hair formed a beard while mud from the mire covered the rest of the face. A look of fear suddenly appeared in his eyes as he peered in the darkness.

I jumped forward and Sir Henry followed. Selden screamed a curse when he saw us, and he heaved a rock in our direction. Then he sprang to his feet and began to run down the hillside.

I could have used my revolver, but I had brought it to defend myself, not to shoot an unarmed man.

Even though Sir Henry and I are in good physical condition, Selden was as swift as a mountain goat, and we soon lost him.

As we sat down on a rock trying to catch our breath, my eyes traveled across the jagged shapes on the moor. They stopped for an instant on a strange sight. There, on top of one of the large ancient rocks, the one they call Black Tor, I saw

The Convict Attacks!

the figure of a man. He stood with his legs apart, his arms folded, and his head bent. I didn't imagine it, Holmes. I saw it all quite clearly. It was not the convict. This was a much taller man. I turned to grab Sir Henry's arm to point out the man, but, in that instant, he disappeared.

I would have liked to have searched for that stranger, but Sir Henry was still very shaky from the hound's cry, so we decided to return to Baskerville Hall.

So, Holmes, choose what you feel is important from this report, and I shall keep trying to solve these mysteries that keep cropping up on the moor.

WATSON

The Man on Black Tor

Barrymore Is Angry at Sir Henry.

CHAPTER 8

Two New Clues

The following morning, Watson was just returning from mailing his report to Holmes when he heard Barrymore in the library.

"How could you do it, Sir Henry?" he cried. "How could you use the information I gave you to hunt down my brother-in-law?"

"Now hold on there, Barrymore!" interrupted Watson. "Selden is a danger to all the people in the countryside."

But Barrymore pleaded with Sir Henry, "I give you my word, sir, he will not bother anyone around here. I have arranged for him to leave the country soon. I have given him everything he needs—food, money, clothing. He wouldn't be foolish enough to commit a crime and show the police where he was."

Sir Henry thought a moment. "All right, Barrymore," he said. "Just this one time."

"Oh thank you, sir," cried Barrymore. "It would have killed my poor wife if he had been caught again."

Barrymore turned to go, then stopped. "Sir Henry," he began, "you have been so kind to us that I would like to do something for you in return. I have some information about Sir Charles' death that I didn't tell the police because I didn't discover it until after the investigation was over."

Watson jumped to his feet. "Do you know how he died?" he asked.

"No," answered Barrymore, "I just know why he was at the moor gate at that hour. It was to meet a woman!"

Some Surprising News!

"Sir Charles, to meet a woman?" asked Sir Henry in surprise. "Who was she?"

"I don't know her name, sir, only her initials. On the morning of his death, Sir Charles received a letter. As I carried it to him, I could not help but notice that it was addressed in a woman's handwriting and that the postmark was from the town of Coombe Tracey. Anyway, I didn't think any more about the letter until a few weeks ago. I was cleaning out the fireplace and I found the ashes of a burned letter. A small part of the writing at the bottom was untouched. It said, 'Please burn this letter after you read it and be at the moor gate by ten o'clock.' It was signed with the initials, 'L.L.'"

"Do you have any idea who this 'L.L.' is?" asked Watson.

"No sir," said Barrymore.

A Burned Letter

This could be an important clue, thought Watson—one he'd have to check further with Dr. Mortimer when he came by that evening.

"A woman with the initials 'L.L.' who lives nearby?" said Dr. Mortimer, deep in thought over Watson's question. "Why yes! There's Laura Lyons. She's in Coombe Tracey."

Watson felt his excitement grow. The letter had been postmarked Coombe Tracey.

"And just who is Laura Lyons?" he asked.

"You've met old Frankland, the lawyer," said Dr. Mortimer. "Well, she's his daughter. Some time back, she married against her father's wishes and he never forgave her. Her husband turned out no good, and he soon left her. Laura was then forced to find some way to support herself. Sir Charles and Jack Stapleton helped her start a small typing business."

Watson thought about his two new clues, Laura Lyons and the stranger on the moor, as he sat alone in the library after dinner. When

L.L. Is Identified.

Barrymore brought in his coffee, Watson decided to follow one of his leads.

"Tell me, Barrymore, on your trips out to the moor, have you seen any man besides Selden?"

"I haven't, sir," said Barrymore, "but Selden told me there was another man hiding out there too. He saw him a few times near those ancient stone huts on the hillside. He was dressed like a gentleman, which is strange for someone hiding on the moor. And each day, a young boy came out to him with a bundle—food and other supplies, I guess. Do you know who he is, sir?"

Watson shook his head. He was now more determined than ever to find this stranger and get some answers from him.

Barrymore Tells of a Stranger on the Moor.

Watson Meets Laura Lyons.

CHAPTER 9

The Stranger on the Moor

Early the next morning, Watson went into Coombe Tracey to call on Laura Lyons. He introduced himself to the beautiful young woman by explaining that he knew her father.

"I have had nothing to do with my father since my marriage," she said bitterly. "Why, if it weren't for Sir Charles Baskerville and other kind people, I might have starved."

"Then perhaps you will answer some questions I have about Sir Charles," said Watson. "First, did you ever write a letter to him?"

Laura Lyons' eyes blazed. "What right do you have asking me such a question?"

"If I took my information to the police, you might be embarrassed, Mrs. Lyons," said Watson. "Now will you answer my question?"

"All right," she said. "Yes, I did write to Sir Charles a few times. You see, he usually sent me money or typing work through Mr. Stapleton, so I rarely saw him to thank him for his kindness in person."

"Did you ever write to Sir Charles to ask him to meet you?" asked Watson.

"Certainly not!" she cried angrily.

"Not even on the very day of his death?"

"No!"

"Perhaps you have just forgotten, Mrs. Lyons, so let me help you remember. You wrote asking him to meet you at the moor gate at ten o'clock. Then he was to burn your letter. Now do you remember?

Mrs. Lyons turned white. "Yes, yes!" she cried. "I needed a large sum of money. Ever since my

"I Did Write to Sir Charles."

husband left me, he has been making my life miserable. The only way to stop him from bothering me was to get a divorce. I wanted to borrow the money for the divorce from Sir Charles. I believed that if I saw him and asked for the loan in person, he would give it to me."

"Well, what happened when you arrived at the moor gate?" asked Watson.

"I never went," she said. "At the last minute, I got help from someone else."

"Who was that someone else, Mrs. Lyons?"

"I really cannot see where that is your business, Dr. Watson," she said.

Watson was losing his patience. "Mrs. Lyons," he reminded her, "you are going to get into a great deal of trouble by not telling me everything."

But Laura Lyons refused to give him any more information. So Watson left.

As his carriage made its way back to the countryside, it passed Lafter Hall. Mr. Frankland,

Watson Loses His Patience.

standing outside, called to Watson and invited him in for a glass of wine. By stopping here, Watson would have an excuse for sending the carriage away. Then, when he left Frankland, he could head out onto the moor in search of the mysterious stranger.

Frankland was eager for someone to listen to his usual complaints against the local police and how they handled his cases. As the lawyer ranted and raved, Watson stood at the window looking out at the moor in the distance. Was the stranger out there hiding in one of those hundreds of stone huts?

Watson wasn't paying much attention to Frankland until the lawyer said, ". . . but I won't help the police catch him. No sir!"

Watson's eyes lit up. "Catch who?"

"The man on the moor, of course," said Frankland. "It's probably the convict."

"You mean you know where he is?"

Frankland Invites Watson In.

"Not exactly. But I could find him by following the young boy who brings him his food every day. I have seen him through my telescope as he heads out onto the moor with his bundle. Who else would he be bringing it to but the escaped convict?"

Watson was listening carefully now. Maybe his luck was finally changing.

Frankland was saying, "But I'm not going to tell those police any . . ." He stopped and stared out the window. "Wait a minute, I see something moving on the hillside. Come, Watson, come!" he cried as he rushed up the stairs. "You will see with your own eyes through my telescope."

When they reached the roof, Frankland put his eye up to the telescope and called, "Quick, Watson, before he passes over the hill!"

Watson took his place at the telescope and saw a young boy with a bundle on his shoulder. When the boy reached the top of the hill, he looked

Watson Sees a Young Boy on the Hillside.

around as if to make certain he was not being followed. Then he disappeared over the hill.

At that moment, Watson's only thought was to get out of Lafter Hall and follow that boy into the moor. He thanked Frankland for the wine, then set off for the hillside where the boy had disappeared.

The sun was sinking as Watson reached the top. The boy was nowhere to be seen. But as Watson gazed down at the circle of stone huts, his eye stopped at a hut in the middle. It was different from the others. It had part of a roof on it. Just enough to protect someone from the weather!

Watson's heart was pounding so hard as he made his way down the rocky hillside that he couldn't even continue smoking. He threw his cigarette aside and took out his revolver. He approached the opening of the hut and looked in. It was empty!

Watson Approaches the Stone Hut.

But there was proof inside that a man had been living there. Blankets were rolled up on a stone bench and empty food cans lay near a pile of warm ashes.

In the middle of the hut stood a stone slab which seemed to serve as a table. On the stone slab rested the same cloth bundle that the boy had been carrying. Watson opened the bundle and found a loaf of bread, a jar of fruit, and a piece of paper. He raised the paper to his eyes in the dim light and read the rough pencil writing, "DR. WATSON HAS GONE TO COOMBE TRACEY."

Had someone been spying on him all along and reporting his movements to this mysterious stranger? Watson was puzzled. There was nothing in the hut to give him a clue to this man's identity, but Watson had come here to find him, and he would stay until he did.

He sat down in a dark corner of the hut and waited. Fifteen minutes went by, then thirty, then an hour.

A Mysterious Note!

At last, he heard footsteps coming. A boot hit a stone, then another and another, coming nearer and nearer. Watson grasped his revolver tightly and pushed himself against the wall of the hut in the darkness.

There was a long pause—the stranger had stopped walking—then the footsteps began again. In seconds, a shadow fell across the opening of the hut.

"It is a lovely evening, my dear Watson," said a familiar voice. "Why not come outside and join me?"

The Stranger Arrives!

"Holmes! Holmes!"

CHAPTER 10

Death on the Moor

For a moment or two, Watson sat stunned. He couldn't believe his ears. That cold sharp voice could belong to only one person in the entire world.

"Holmes! Holmes!" he cried.

"Come out, Watson," said Mr. Sherlock Holmes, "and please put away your revolver."

Watson rushed outside the hut, and there on a rock sat Sherlock Holmes, smiling. "I was never so glad to see anyone in my whole life," cried Watson joyously.

"Or more surprised, eh?" added Holmes. "But the surprise was not all yours, my dear Watson. I had no idea that you were here until I was a few feet from the hut."

"How did you know it then?" asked Watson.

"My dear fellow, if you really want to fool me, you'll have to change your brand of cigarettes. When I see the stub of a cigarette marked, 'Bradley, Oxford Street,' I know that my friend, Watson, is close by. It is there on the path where you threw it before you charged into the empty hut."

"Exactly!" answered Watson.

"And knowing you, I was certain that you were sitting inside with your revolver ready. But tell me, Watson, how did you know where to look for me? Did you see me standing on that black rock the night you were chasing the escaped convict?"

"Yes, I saw you then," admitted Watson, "but your delivery boy was also seen."

Watson's Cigarette Gave Him Away.

"By the old gentleman with the telescope, no doubt," said Holmes. "I have seen the sunlight flashing on the lens and guessed that perhaps he was watching me."

"He was," said Watson. "But tell me, Holmes, when did you get here and what have you been doing? I thought you were still working on another case in London."

"That's exactly what I wanted you to think," said Holmes.

Watson looked disappointed. "Didn't you trust me enough to tell me your plans?"

"My dear fellow," said Holmes, "please forgive me if it seems that I tricked you. But if I had come here with you and Sir Henry, our enemy would have been on guard. This way, I have been able to find out what I needed to without being known. I brought a lad with me from London to bring me what I needed."

Holmes got up and went inside the hut. "Aha! I see my supplies are here. And what's this paper?

Holmes Finds His Supplies.

So you have been to Coombe Tracey, Watson. To see Laura Lyons?"

"Why yes," said Watson. He told Holmes the story of his visit to the young woman. Holmes was so interested that he had Watson repeat the story twice.

"That answers many questions for me," said Holmes. "Were you aware, Watson, that Laura Lyons is very much in love with Jack Stapleton? They meet often, they write to each other, and they have made plans to be married. I plan to use this information when I talk to his wife . . ."

"His wife?" Watson was stunned.

"Yes, my dear fellow. The lady who is known as his sister is really his wife."

"Good Heavens, Holmes!" cried Watson. "Why did he pretend she was his sister?"

"Because he hoped to use her as a single woman to attract the Baskerville men. You see, Watson, Jack Stapleton is our enemy. He is the bearded man who followed Sir Henry in London."

Watson Learns of Stapleton's Wife!

"And the warning note Sir Henry received?" asked Watson.

"That came from Beryl Stapleton. You see, Watson, I became suspicious after reading one of your reports. Stapleton really trapped himself without knowing it when he gave you information about the school he once owned in Yorkshire. I was able to trace him there. I found that the descriptions of the schoolmaster and his wife matched exactly what you had told me about Jack and Beryl Stapleton."

Watson was still puzzled. "But if this woman is his wife, where does Laura Lyons fit in?"

"Aha, Watson. This is where you have been of great help. You found out that Mrs. Lyons was planning to divorce her husband. I am certain that she counted on Jack Stapleton marrying her."

"And when she finds out the truth?"

Holmes Traces Stapleton's School.

"Why then I'm hoping that Mrs. Lyons will be very willing to help us."

"One last question, Holmes. What is Stapleton after? Why would he want to kill off all the Baskervilles?"

"I don't know that yet, Watson. All I know is that this is a case of cold-blooded planned murder. But enough talk! It is getting late, and you must return to Baskerville Hall to be with Sir Henry."

As Watson got up to leave, a terrible scream broke the silence of the moor. "Oh my God!" he gasped. "What was that?"

Holmes jumped to his feet and ran outside.

The screams continued, getting nearer and nearer, louder and louder.

Then a new sound followed the terrible screams—a low moan, growing into a roar, then back to a moan again.

"It's the hound!" cried Holmes. "Hurry, Watson, before we are too late!"

A Terrible Scream Is Heard!

As they started to run, they heard one last yell, then a thud. Then silence! They ran blindly through the darkness, forcing their way through bushes, slamming into rocks, heading in the direction where they had heard the cries.

Suddenly, a low moan came to them from a rocky slope on their left. Something dark seemed to be spread out on the ground.

As Holmes and Watson came closer to it, they saw it was the body of a man. His head was twisted under him as if he were in the middle of a somersault. But not a moan, not a whisper, not a movement came from the body.

Holmes lit a match. He and Watson gasped. The man's crushed skull lay in a spreading pool of blood. As their eyes traveled over the body, they both froze in shock. It was Sir Henry Baskerville!

Rushing Towards the Screams

There could be no mistake about that brown tweed suit and the matching hat that lay beside the body. It was the very same outfit that Sir Henry had worn that morning he visited them in London.

The match flickered out. Watson shook his fists and cried, "I shall never forgive myself for leaving him alone tonight."

"I am more to blame than you," groaned Holmes. "But how could I know that he would disobey my orders and come out on the moor alone? Just wait until I get my hands on that Stapleton! I swear I . . ."

"Can't we simply go get him now?"

"That fellow is clever, Watson. We know he's using that hound to murder, but we have to be able to prove it," said Holmes as he bent down to examine the body.

Suddenly, he jumped up laughing. He danced around Watson, shaking his hand.

"Have you gone mad, Holmes?" cried Watson.

It's Sir Henry Baskerville!

"A beard, Watson! A beard! The man has a beard." Holmes turned the body over. "See, Watson! It is not Sir Henry at all. It is Neil Selden, the escaped convict."

"Of course, Holmes," said Watson. "Now I remember. Sir Henry gave his old clothes to Barrymore, and Barrymore probably gave some of them to Selden to help him escape. The shirt, the suit, the cap—they were all Sir Henry's."

"Then the clothes were the cause of his death," said Holmes. "The hound was given some of Sir Henry's clothing to smell—probably the boot that was stolen from the hotel in London. With the scent of that boot, the hound was able to follow this poor man."

"What puzzles me, Holmes, is why the hound was loose tonight. Did Stapleton expect Sir Henry to be on the moor at this hour?" asked Watson.

"Have You Gone Mad, Holmes?"

"We won't have to wait long to find out," answered Holmes. "Look there, Watson. Our Mr. Stapleton is heading right for us. We must not let him know that we are suspicious of him or my plans will be ruined."

The moon shone on Jack Stapleton as he walked across the moor. The red glow of a cigar in his mouth lit up his smiling face.

"Why, Dr. Watson!" he exclaimed. "I hardly expected to see you on the moor at this hour. But what's this? Is somebody hurt? Don't tell me it's Sir Henry!"

Stapleton hurried past the two men and bent over the body. He gasped, and the cigar dropped from his fingers. "Wh-who is this?" he stammered.

"It is the escaped convict, Selden," answered Watson.

Stapleton turned white, but he tried to cover his shock. "Dear me! How terrible! How did he die?"

Stapleton Discovers His Mistake.

"He probably fell over these rocks and broke his neck," said Holmes. "Watson and I were out for a walk and we heard his cry."

"I heard the cry also," said Stapleton. "That's why I came out. I was worried about Sir Henry."

Aha, thought Holmes, now we'll find out! "Why should you be worried about Sir Henry being out here on the moor tonight?"

"Because I had invited him to dinner. When he didn't come, I became alarmed. Then, when I heard cries on the moor, I came running out. But I didn't expect to meet the great Mr. Sherlock Holmes," said Stapleton with a bow to the detective.

"You are very quick at recognizing me," said Holmes.

"We have been expecting you ever since Dr. Watson arrived," said Stapleton.

"Why, thank you," said Holmes, "but I'm afraid my visit must be quite short, for I must return to London tomorrow."

Stapleton Recognizes the Great Mr. Holmes.

"Have you found any answers yet to Sir Henry's problems?" asked Stapleton.

"A detective needs facts to solve a case," explained Holmes. "Legends about ghostly hounds do not count. No, I fear that I have failed in this case."

Stapleton breathed a sigh of relief at Holmes' words. Then he changed the subject. "Shall we cover this poor chap and leave him out here until we can call the police in the morning?"

Holmes and Watson agreed, and the men separated. Holmes and Watson headed back towards Baskerville Hall and Stapleton, to Merripit House.

Once again, the moor was silent. The only movement now was the fluttering of a bird as it circled over a dark spot on the rocky slope of the moor.

Stapleton Covers the Body.

"Say Nothing About the Hound!"

CHAPTER 11

Setting the Trap

"Can't we arrest him now?" asked Watson as he and Holmes walked across the moor.

"My dear Watson, we still have no proof. We would be laughed out of any court if we came in with a story about a killer hound and a body with no teeth marks. But even more important, we don't know Stapleton's reasons for the murders."

When they reached Baskerville Hall, Holmes warned Watson, "Say nothing to Sir Henry about the hound. For now, I want him to believe that Selden's death was simply from the fall. I need

Sir Henry strong and calm for tomorrow when, according to your report, he is dining with the Stapletons at their house."

Sir Henry welcomed Holmes to Baskerville Hall and proudly explained how well he had kept his promise. "I have been quite bored spending the evening here all alone. I was almost tempted to visit Merripit House when Stapleton sent over an invitation earlier, but I remembered my promise to you not to go out alone, so I did not leave the Hall."

Holmes and Watson exchanged glances. So that was how Stapleton had planned to lure Sir Henry out onto the moor tonight!

Holmes then told Sir Henry about Selden's death. But, in the middle of the story, Holmes stopped. His eyes were glued to the library wall. "These are some very fine paintings, Sir Henry," he said excitedly.

"Well, I'm glad to hear you say so," said Sir Henry. He was surprised at Holmes' sudden

Holmes Admires the Paintings.

interest in art when Selden's death seemed so much more important to discuss.

"These are family portraits, are they not?" asked Holmes.

"Yes," said Sir Henry, going over to one of the portraits. "This is Admiral John Baskerville, who sailed the West Indies. And this is Sir William Baskerville, who was a member of the House of Commons. And this fellow in the black velvet suit, the lace collar, and the long yellow curls is the one who caused all this trouble. That's the wicked Hugo who started the legend of the Hound of the Baskervilles."

Watson stared at the portrait in amazement. "Dear me!" he exclaimed, "he seems so quiet and easygoing. It's hard to believe he was such an evil man."

Holmes didn't say anything more about Hugo's portrait, but all through dinner, his eyes were glued to it.

The Wicked Hugo Baskerville

Once Sir Henry had gone up to bed, Holmes went back to the portrait and called to Watson. "Do you see anything here, Watson? Is it like anyone you know?"

Watson studied the wide hat, the long curling hair, and the straight, serious face with its thin lips and cold grey eyes. "There seems to be a little of Sir Henry in the shape of the jaw," he said.

"Perhaps!" said Holmes as he pulled a chair to the wall and climbed on it. He curved his right arm over the painting of Hugo so it covered the hat and the hair.

"Good Heavens!" cried Watson in amazement. "It's the face of Jack Stapleton! Why, this might be his very own portrait."

"Yes," said Holmes. "Jack Stapleton is a Baskerville—that's for sure. He not only inherited Hugo's looks, but his evil soul as well."

"So his plan was to get his hands on the Baskerville estate?" said Watson.

"It's the Face of Jack Stapleton!"

"Exactly!" said Holmes. "This picture has answered my most puzzling question—why Stapleton wanted Sir Charles and Sir Henry dead. We have him now, Watson, and I swear to you that before tomorrow is over, this case will be closed."

The following morning, Holmes began setting the trap. First, he said to Sir Henry, "I understand, sir, that you have plans to dine at the Stapletons' home this evening."

Sir Henry nodded. "And I hope you and Watson will join me," he replied.

"I'm afraid that's not possible," said Holmes. "You see, Watson and I must leave for London this afternoon."

Sir Henry's face dropped. "London? I thought you were going to stay here until this case was solved," he said glumly.

"My dear fellow," said Holmes, "please trust me. I just might be able to solve this case if I can

Holmes Announces His Return to London.

have your help. Are you willing to do anything I ask and not question my reasons why?"

Sir Henry looked puzzled, but agreed. "I will do whatever you say, Mr. Holmes."

"Fine!" said Holmes. "First, you will keep your dinner plans. But you must explain to the Stapletons that Watson and I had important business in London and that we hope to return here in a day or two. Now, will you remember to tell them that?"

"Of course," said Sir Henry.

"Next," added Holmes, "I want you to drive to Merripit House, then send your driver and carriage back here. But be sure to let the Stapletons know you plan to walk home across the moor."

"You want me to walk across the moor alone at night?" cried Sir Henry. "But that's the very thing you have warned me not to do."

Sir Henry Can't Believe His Ears!

"This time, I assure you, Sir Henry, you will be perfectly safe," said Holmes. "Just be sure you walk along the main path!"

"All right," sighed Sir Henry.

A short while later, Holmes and Watson said good-bye to Sir Henry and headed for Coombe Tracey. But instead of boarding the train, Holmes turned and walked away from the railway station.

"Come along, Watson," he called. "We are going to call upon Mrs. Laura Lyons."

"You mean we're not going to London?" asked Watson. Then suddenly, he knew exactly what Holmes was planning. If Sir Henry could convince Stapleton that Holmes and Watson had really gone to London, then Stapleton might feel free to act. But they would still be here, close enough to protect Sir Henry.

Laura Lyons was at her typewriter when Holmes and Watson entered. Holmes began questioning her about Sir Charles' death.

"We're Not Going to London?"

"Dr. Watson tells me that there is some information you refused to give him."

"And I still refuse," she said angrily.

Holmes' voice turned hard. "I believe, Mrs. Lyons, that the meeting you planned with Sir Charles led to his death. This is a case of murder, and we may find that not only are you a part of it, but so is Jack Stapleton. And so is his wife!"

Mrs. Lyons jumped up. "His wife?"

Holmes sat back in his chair and smiled. Her reaction was exactly what he had hoped it would be. "Yes, Mrs. Lyons," he said slowly, "the woman who has been calling herself his sister is really his wife."

"But he can't be married!" she gasped.

"I have come here prepared to prove it," said Holmes as he took some papers from his pocket. "Here is a picture of the two of them taken four years ago before they came here and changed

Laura Learns of Stapleton's Wife!

their name. It is marked, 'Mr. and Mrs. Vandeleur,' but you can see it is them. And here are letters from three different people who knew them when they ran their school in Yorkshire."

Laura Lyons fell into a chair and spoke weakly. "I can see now that this man lied to me, but I will not lie for him any longer. Ask me whatever you wish, and I swear to tell the truth. But, believe one thing—when I wrote to Sir Charles, I never dreamed it would harm him. He was my kindest friend."

"I know how painful this must be," said Holmes, "so I will try to make it easier by telling you what I know; then you can add whatever you know. First, Stapleton was the one who suggested you write the letter."

"Yes, he told me what to write, word for word. He said Sir Charles would surely give me the money if I asked him in person."

"Then, after you sent the letter, he persuaded you not to keep the appointment."

Laura Recognizes the Vandeleurs.

"Yes, he said his pride would be hurt if he let another man help me. He promised to give me the money himself. So I didn't go."

"And then you heard nothing more until you read of Sir Charles' death in the newspapers."

"That's correct. That's when Jack warned me not to say anything. He said the death was mysterious, and if the police found out I was supposed to meet Sir Charles, they would suspect me."

Watson and Holmes thanked Mrs. Lyons for her help, then got up to leave.

"And now, my dear Watson," said Holmes as the door closed behind them, "we shall head directly for our trap on the moor."

Holmes Thanks Laura Lyons.

Setting a Trap at Merripit House

CHAPTER 12

The Hound of the Baskervilles

As Holmes' carriage neared Merripit House, he had the driver stop partway down the road. Holmes and Watson got off.

"Have your revolver ready, Watson," said Holmes. "The lights of the house are just ahead of us. We must walk softly and speak only in whispers."

They tiptoed along the path, and when they were about two hundred yards from the house, Holmes stopped. "These rocks on the side of the path will hide us quite well. Now Watson, creep forward quietly to those lighted windows and see what's going on inside."

Watson tiptoed down the path and hid behind a low stone wall. Inside, he could see Jack Stapleton and Sir Henry seated at the dining room table. Stapleton was talking brightly, but Sir Henry sat silent and pale. He's probably thinking about that lonely walk back home across the moor, thought Watson.

Then Stapleton got up from his chair and left the room. In a few moments, Watson heard a door creak. Then footsteps sounded on the gravel nearby.

Watson peered over the wall and saw Stapleton heading for a small shed in the corner of the yard. He turned a key in the lock and went inside. A curious growling sound came from inside the shed, but in a minute, Stapleton came out and locked the shed behind him. Then he went back into the house.

Sir Henry and Stapleton Are Together.

Watson returned to Holmes and reported what he had seen.

"Wasn't Mrs. Stapleton there?" asked Holmes.

"There wasn't a sign of her in the dining room or in the kitchen," said Watson.

"Where can she be?" Holmes puzzled.

But at that moment, a new problem was becoming more important. The fog from out in the mire was slowly heading towards the path. It was so thick that it looked like a sheet of ice with the moon shining on it.

"This could be serious, Watson," said Holmes. "If that fog keeps moving towards us, it could cover the path and block our view. The success of my plan and even Sir Henry's life now depend on his starting for home before the fog gets any thicker and any closer."

After about fifteen minutes, the sound of quick footsteps broke the silence on the moor. The steps

Fog Covers the Path.

grew louder, but Holmes and Watson saw nothing but fog on the path. Then suddenly, through the curtain of fog, stepped Sir Henry. He was walking quickly and glancing back over his shoulder every few seconds.

"Get ready, Watson," cried Holmes in a loud whisper. "It's coming!"

The noise of pattering feet was coming from somewhere inside that curtain of fog. Holmes and Watson both had their revolvers ready as they gazed anxiously at the path.

Then suddenly, they jerked forward and their lips parted in amazement. A dreadful shape was moving out of the fog. It was a huge coal-black hound, but unlike any hound they had ever seen. Fire burst from its open mouth, its eyes glowed with a ghostly shine, and its muzzle and collar were outlined in a gleaming fire. Never in their wildest dreams had Holmes and Watson ever seen anything more frightening or savage.

The Hound Closes In.

They froze for an instant, but when they saw that the hound was leaping down the path after Sir Henry, they fired together.

The creature gave a strange howl, but continued running. The sound of the shots made Sir Henry whirl around. His face turned white and he raised his hands in horror. He stood helpless as the savage beast came at him.

Holmes and Watson ran out from behind the rock and onto the path. But before they could reach Sir Henry, the beast had leaped upon him and thrown him to the ground.

In a flash, Holmes emptied five bullets into the hound's side. With a howl of pain and a snap of its whole body, the giant hound rolled on its back and then was still.

From where he lay on the ground, Sir Henry whispered weakly, "My God! What was it?"

Holmes Fires!

"Whatever it is, it's dead," said Holmes. "We've done away with the family ghost once and for all."

Holmes and Watson stared down at the creature lying at their feet. The huge powerful hound was almost the size of a lion. Even in death, its jaws seemed to be dripping a blue flame, and the small, cruel eyes had rings of fire around them.

Watson bent over and touched the glowing muzzle. His fingers shone in the darkness. "It's just a paste made of phosphorus so it would glow in the dark," he explained. "How utterly clever!"

"Yes, Watson," said Holmes, "that man is quite clever trying to make the hound look ghostly. But he's not clever enough to outwit Sherlock Holmes."

Holmes helped Sir Henry to his feet and added, "We must apologize to you, Sir Henry, for having put you in such danger."

Phosphorus Paste That Glows in the Dark!

"But you saved my life, the two of you," he answered weakly.

"And now we must find Stapleton," said Holmes. "The shots probably warned him and he already may have tried to escape."

They left Sir Henry resting on a rock and rushed to the house. Holmes grabbed a lamp and they began to search every room. When they came to a locked door on the second floor, Watson cried out, "There's someone in there. I heard some movement."

With their revolvers ready, Holmes and Watson kicked open the door and burst in. In the center of the room stood an old tall beam, placed there to hold up a sagging roof. Tied to this beam was a figure so completely wrapped in sheets that they couldn't make out who it was.

Watson immediately began unwrapping the moaning figure, and in a minute, Mrs. Beryl Stapleton fell to the floor at his feet.

Holmes and Watson Kick Open the Door.

"Is he safe?" she gasped. "Has he escaped?"

"Your husband cannot escape us, madam," said Holmes coldly.

"No, no," protested the woman. "I meant Sir Henry. Is he safe?"

"Yes," answered Watson.

"And the hound?" she asked fearfully.

"It is dead," said Holmes.

She gave a long sigh. "Thank God! See how that horrible man has treated me," she cried, pushing up her sleeves to show them her bruised arms. "I tried to live a lie for him because I believed he loved me, but now I know the truth about his murderous plans." She began to sob.

"Since you have helped him with his evil work, madam," said Holmes, "you had better make up for it now by telling us where he is."

Watson Frees Mrs. Stapleton.

"His only hiding place would be the island in the middle of the mire," she said. "Nobody could ever get to it." Then she began to laugh wildly. "But with the fog so thick tonight, he may never get to it either."

Holmes and Watson realized that they could never follow Stapleton through the mire until the fog had lifted. So they returned to Sir Henry and took him back to Baskerville Hall to get over his fright.

The next morning brought sunshine to the moor. Mrs. Stapleton took Holmes and Watson to Grimpen Mire and led them across the path her husband used to get to the island in the middle.

As they were stepping across the dark shaking mud, Holmes saw something sticking up among the rotting plants. He reached down into the thick slime and came up with an old black boot. On the inside, he could make out the writing, "Dunne's, New York." It was Sir Henry's missing boot—the one he had brought with him from

Crossing Grimpen Mire

America, the one which had been stolen from the hotel in London.

"We now know that Stapleton must have come this way," said Holmes. "He probably used this boot to give the hound Sir Henry's scent. Then, as he fled across the mire, he must have thrown it in here."

Holmes and Watson searched every corner of the island, but Stapleton was nowhere to be found.

"He probably never even made it across the mire in that fog," said Holmes. "And there aren't even any fresh footprints here."

Watson looked out at the thick foul-smelling mud. "Then Holmes, he's . . ."

"Yes, Watson," said Holmes grimly, "somewhere down at the bottom of this huge slimy mire, that cruel, evil man is buried."

Sir Henry's Missing Boot

Holmes Begins His Story.

CHAPTER 13

The Amazing Mr. Holmes

The following morning, Sherlock Holmes explained to Watson and Sir Henry how he had solved the case.

"Now that I have checked everything completely, gentlemen, I have all the answers for you. This fellow who called himself Stapleton was really a Baskerville. He was the son of Sir Charles' brother, Rodger, the one who had fled to South America. Even though the family believed he died unmarried, the truth is he did marry and have a son. This son, also named Rodger, stole a large sum of money in South America. Then he changed his name to Vandeleur and fled with his wife, Beryl, to England.

"They set up a private school in Yorkshire, but it failed. Vandeleur took the school's money and fled again.

"Then he changed his name once more, this time to Stapleton. He probably checked family records and found that only two people stood between him and the valuable Baskerville estate. So he moved to the moor to carry out his murderous plans.

"There, Stapleton learned that Sir Charles had a weak heart and also that he believed in the legend of the hound completely. That gave him the idea for a murder where everyone would blame the Baskerville family curse.

"I found the dealer in London where he bought the dog. It was the most savage beast they ever sold. He had the dog shipped to him in a closed carriage so no one would see it. Then he hid it on his secret island in the mire.

Holmes Locates the Dog Dealer.

"When Mrs. Stapleton discovered her husband was planning Sir Charles' murder, she refused to help him. Pretending to be his sister was one thing, but murder was another. That's when he decided to use Laura Lyons. He was sure that if he got her to fall in love with him, she would do anything he asked, like getting a divorce and using Sir Charles for the money.

"She agreed to write the letter asking Sir Charles to meet her. Then, on the day of the meeting, Stapleton visited Mrs. Lyons and persuaded her not to go by promising to give her the money himself.

"He returned home, got the hound, put the phosphorus paste on it, and took it to the moor gate to wait for Sir Charles.

"When Stapleton ordered the dog to attack, it jumped over the moor gate and chased Sir Charles down Yew Alley. The hound probably ran

The Hound Attacks Sir Charles.

on the grass, so that is why none of its footprints were found on the dirt path.

"But when the hound reached Sir Charles, the old man was already dead from his heart attack. Since hounds do not attack dead bodies, it simply turned away. But in turning, it left the footprints we found.

"With Sir Charles out of the way, Stapleton turned his attention to Sir Henry. He had no difficulty finding out the details of Sir Henry's arrival from Dr. Mortimer. So he went to London, probably hoping to kill Sir Henry there, but something stopped him. You see, Stapleton knew that he could no longer trust his wife alone, not after she refused to help him murder Sir Charles. So he locked her in their hotel room while he put on a beard and followed Sir Henry.

"When Sir Henry and Dr. Mortimer led him to 221B Baker Street, he discovered he was up against the world's expert in solving crime,

Hounds Do Not Attack Dead Bodies.

Mr. Sherlock Holmes. So he probably gave up the idea of murdering Sir Henry in London.

"Meanwhile, Mrs. Stapleton felt she had to warn Sir Henry of her husband's plans. But she feared the man so, she couldn't take the chance of writing a letter in her own handwriting. So she cut the words from a newspaper and addressed the envelope in rough printed letters.

"You may remember, Watson, that when Sir Henry showed me the letter for the first time, I held it up close to my face. What I was doing was smelling the paper, for I had noticed a faint scent of perfume. That led me to believe the writer was a woman.

"Then we get to the matter of the scent for the hound. Stapleton had to find some way of giving the hound Sir Henry's scent. He probably stole the first boot from outside Sir Henry's room. But it was the new brown boot which Sir Henry had

Mrs. Stapleton Cuts Out Her Letter.

not worn yet. So it had no scent. Stapleton then had to return that boot and steal another—this time, the old black one. This gave me a clue that we were dealing with a real hound who could pick up a scent, and not some supernatural beast.

"I came to the moor in secret because I was almost certain by then that Stapleton was our man. I knew I had to watch him, but I could not have done this if I were at Baskerville Hall. For then, Stapleton would surely have been on his guard.

"From my hut on the moor, I was able to watch everybody. The lad I brought with me from London supplied me with everything I needed, including your reports, Watson, as they were forwarded to him from London. Your report on Stapleton's school led me to the discovery of exactly who he was.

"So even though I knew all this when you found me on the moor, I still had no real proof. I had to

Holmes Receives Watson's Reports.

catch Stapleton red-handed. And to do this, I had to use you, Sir Henry, as bait in my trap.

"On the day you were expected for dinner, Sir Henry, Mrs. Stapleton saw the hound being prepared in the shed. She accused her husband of planning your murder that night, and a terrible fight followed. Stapleton feared she would warn you, so he tied her in an upstairs room. He probably hoped that once you were out of the way and he had all the Baskerville millions, he could win her back. For surely, everyone would blame your death on the family curse, just as they did Sir Charles' death. Then he would be in the clear.

"Now, gentlemen, do you have any questions?"

"Just one, Mr. Holmes," said Sir Henry. "I am a strong, healthy young man with a perfectly good heart. How could Stapleton have hoped to frighten me to death as he did my uncle?"

You Will Not Warn Sir Henry!

"Stapleton starved the hound for several days so that it would go after any flesh when he ordered it to attack," explained Holmes.

"Holmes, you amaze me!" cried Watson, "but then you always do."

"There's no need for praise, my dear fellow, for Sherlock Holmes is a specialist in solving crimes. And now that I have solved the Case of the Hound of the Baskervilles, with your help, of course, Watson, we must prepare to leave for London in the morning. A new case there awaits my expert talents!"

The Specialist in Solving Crimes